He Shall Live and Not Die:

My Encounter

Leon Rondre Williams

Copyright 2001

ISBN: 978-0-9881753-1-0

AMC World, LLC

" . . . One scientist has told
me that the first few weeks after
birth is the most important period,
for during that time, the child's
brain is enlarging. During that
period, the mother's touch or that
of someone who is acting like a
mother is crucial...."

-Dalai Lama's Book of Wisdom, p. 85

ABOUT THE AUTHOR

Leon Rondre Williams Jr. was born at The Bradley Memorial Hospital in Cleveland Tennessee to his proud parents Leon Sr. (49) and Cheryl Williams (45) of Freeport, Grand Bahamas in 1976. He is the eldest of five children, Chene & Chante 22 (twins), Chanika 19, and his youngest sibling, Lebronze 18.

Rondre –the name he is affectionately known by, started school in 1981 at St. Paul's Methodist College in Grand Bahama, and graduated in 1994.

He then went on to get his **Bachelor's of Science** degree in Electronics Engineering Technology at DeVry Institute of Technology in Atlanta where he graduated Magna cum Laude (3.61 g.p.a).

While at DeVry, Rondre held the position as *Lead Faculty Assistant* where he had direct supervision of nineteen people, and tutored all general education courses as well as most electronic related courses.

Rondre also served as **Vice President of the National Society of Black engineers (*NSBE*)**, treasurer for **Tau Alpha Pi (*Honors Society for engineers*)**, Mentor with the **L.I.N.K.** program (***Leadership Innovators Negotiating Knowledge***), and member of the **Controls** and **Communications Society** of the **IEEE**, (**Institute of Electrical and Electronic Engineers**).

While schooling in Atlanta, Rondre also served as Assistant Youth Leader to Mrs. Ruth Allen at the Church of God of Prophecy, Flatshoals under the leadership of Pastor Levi Thompson.

After graduation, October 24, 1997 Rondre returned home to Freeport where he looked for a job, he was unsuccessful but later, got a job with Northern Telecom (NORTEL, Florida) with the position of Sales & Marketing in which he started on the 16th of February 1998. During the month of March 1998, Rondre received an evaluation at work performed by his direct managers, Mr. Tony Huggins and Mr. Stan Phillips. Rondre failed the evaluation drastically.

Later that week, his mother Cheryl flew from Freeport to Ft. Lauderdale to check on him. The Next day they went to the hospital and Rondre was diagnosed with a life threatening, brain tumor, and was given a sentence of three months to live.

Rondre now serves as Project Manager for Xerox (Bahamas Copier and Office Products Limited) located in Nassau Bahamas, and is the Assistant Youth leader to Mrs. Christine Gibson, under the Pastoral leadership of Bishop Samuel Alleyne.

Chapter One: Growing Up

As a child growing up, the church and its activities engulfed me. Some of the church activities included attending Sunday school, Sunday Morning Worship Service, Sunday Evening Service, Wednesday Night Bible Study, Choir or Musicians Rehearsals, and Youth Service.

One of the main factors that contributed to my church involvement is due to the positions my parents and grandparents held in church. For example, my father was and still is a certified teacher of the scripture so he spent a lot of his free time after work at church teaching. My mother is a lay minister and served as choir director for many, long years. My dad's father, Franklin Williams, has been a Pastor, Bishop, and Overseer. My mom's father, Rufus Bernard Finlayson, has also been a Pastor, Bishop, and Overseer.

So as a child I could not help but being involved in church activities. I loved it at times, but being a normal child, I hated it at times, especially whenever I had to miss a favorite show because it conflicted with the time service started at church.

Train a child in the way he should go, and when
he is old he will not turn from it.
-Proverbs 22: 6

After school, mummy and daddy would hold discussions where we had to tell them how our day at school went. My days in elementary (grade) school went by fairly well. By grade five I had won an award for spelling and in grade six went on to represent the school in a district spelling competition. However, by the time I got to my middle school grades, things changed dramatically.

One day while in grade seven the school had to call daddy in because I accumulated fifteen detentions in one year. Later that day, mummy beat me so bad and told me, "One more detention from you and I will beat you naked in the front of your class." I don't know about the rest of my siblings, but whenever mummy talked, I listened.

"Pleasure that is obtained by unreasonable and unsuitable cost must always end in pain."
– Samuel Johnson {1709-1784 British Author}

–

For some reason, I managed to go straight through the twelfth grade with getting only one demerit. This accomplishment did not come easy or without a price. Consequently, I would take beatings from my mother on a daily basis. Those stripes made me the man I am today (yeah right).

You can have anything you want -- if you want it badly enough. You can be anything you want to be, do anything you set out to accomplish if you hold to that desire with singleness of purpose.
-Abraham Lincoln

I only took two beatings from my daddy, and for some reason I don't think that I would have been able to take anymore. One of my beatings was because I lent my bicycle out to a friend without permission.

The punishment was because I played sick for church and once everyone left for church I went with my neighbor to his church. Now I was supposed to be home before my parents, but for

> *A wise son heeds his father's instruction,*
> *but a mocker does not listen to rebuke.*
> *- Proverbs 13: 1 [NIV]*

some reason, I have yet to find out, I met them home waiting for me to arrive. I don't think I need to say what happened next but I will let you imagine. If you spare the rod you spoil the childand for some reason or the other I don't think I have a spoiled bone in my body.

For the most part, I remember many of the happy times we shared together as a family. Our family had a regular routine that we followed religiously during breakfast and dinner on the weekends. At the table on Saturday morning breakfasts and Sunday afternoon dinners, we would pray and each one of us had to say a verse of scripture that we memorized. This was real fun.

And that from a child thou hast known the holy scriptures, which are able to make thee wise unto salvation through faith which is in Christ Jesus.

- 2 Timothy 3:15

In addition, we had devotions and bible study times regularly. If we didn't have time for devotion in the house, we would have it in the car. My friends' thought it was stupid but none of my parents' have lost interest in the church today. We all take active rolls when possible in a variety of church functions.

"We are not yet what we shall be, but we grow toward it; The process is not yet finished, but is still going on; This life is not the end, it is the way to a better. All does not yet shine with glory; nevertheless, all is being purified."

-Martin Luther

Remember your Creator in the days of your youth, before the days of trouble come and the years approach when you will say, "I find no pleasure in them"

— Ecclesiastes 12:1 [NIV]

—

Chapter Two: College Time

After graduating from high school in 1994, I went to DeVry Institute of Technology in Atlanta later that year to pursue a Bachelor's of Science degree in Electronics Engineering Technology. During my first semester there, I received a 4.0g.p.a. I did not know what to do with myself. I was so happy; I didn't know what to do with myself.

However, three weeks before finals of my second semester I got a painful enlargement of some kind on my left eye. The Doctors could not tell what had happened or why. Each time I studied I cried because of the pressure I felt when I held my head down to read. The pain was unbearable at times. Even more painful was the comments made by a few of professors.

> There is no education like adversity.
>
> *Proverbs 24:10*
>
> *If you falter in times of trouble, how small is your strength*

At that time, a few of my professors didn't want me in their classes. One professor announced his disgust by shouting out in front of my class, "Don't bring that stuff around here, I don't wanna catch nothin'." I had to leave. I was shamed and embarrassed.

Later that day, a friend of mine came over and saw the condition my eye was in. She offered to bring me to the emergency room if the condition worsened. By the time the evening rolled in, I was surrounded with a host of classmates like Jason, Jamal and Housain – to name a few. They attend the same class and brought over the review notes from the lecture I missed.

Consequently, I knew many of the answers to the review questions, but was not allowed to take the test at the same time as the other students until I received a doctor's note diagnosing my current condition. While my friends from school were about to take the exam that Friday, I sat at home on the verge of receiving a zero grade. I didn't let my professors get me down or stop me from going on with my daily routine and plans. The one thing I didn't need both my eyes to do is to play drums. A friend of mine in Atlanta was instrumental in setting up a studio gig on Saturday morning at Mission Recording Studios. Asides from God and my family, playing drums was my life, therefore I was very excited about the opportunity to play drums on an album project. I didn't know the band or artist, but I would be paid for the session work, so I was determined to do the gig whether I could see clearly or not. It was a fun experience and my timing was great that day.

Toward the end of the session, D. J. Lewis – the engineer could not refrain from commenting about my eye. He said, "Did you get into a fight or something? Your eye looks pretty bad man. You need to get that checked out."

Being relatively a new resident to Georgia, I was unfamiliar with the procedures required to obtain a doctor's diagnosis. Even though I planned to attend church Sunday morning, I decided to stay at home. I couldn't bear being seen by anyone else. Right about the time when I began to really think about my eye, school and my

G.P.A., I heard a knock on the door. My friend in Atlanta came over to check on the enlargement. It was Sunday afternoon and she noticed I was not at church that day. When she saw my eye, she concluded that I needed to go to the emergency room and that she was going to take me there. So my friend and my roommate Gregory – also a Bahamian, accompanied me to Dekalb Medical Center. I waited for about an hour or two before I was seen. My friend had to leave so my roommate and I stayed.

The emergency room doctor referred me to a specialist whose office was walking distance from school. I was able to get a doctor's diagnosis and a note for my professor in order to take the exam. I was relieved of 50% of the worry and frustration I felt throughout the ordeal. With lots of prayers, faith, and the power of the Almighty, I got an A on the test, I received a 3.91 g.p.a., that semester adding to a cumulative g.p.a. of 3.94.

GOD IS GOOD ALL THE TIME, AND ALL THE TIME GOD IS GOOD.

I say I was relieved of 50% because when I went to my doctor's appointment, he extracted more than 16 ounces of a puss-like fluid from my eye. The Doctor could not tell me what I had or why I had it. When I think about the overall events that have happened in my life, I wondered if the enlargement in my eye was a warning sign of events to come.

Time was against me; I needed a mighty, powerful act from my Father and Creator.

Throughout my last year in school, I suffered from severe migraine headaches. But I didn't let it hinder the fun I planned on having during my last year. I had the opportunity to play drums in a Junkanoo Parade at Tuskegee, AL with my friend Everette. I traveled a lot with my friends and family to places like Lakeland and Orlando FL, Columbus, GA and to the National NSBE convention in 1997.

I remember playing basketball with my friends in August during my last semester. It was the best I played in my life. I went up to the basket for a lay up, I won't call any names but my good friend Jason Taylor bridged me and I came down on my left arm and broke my wrist.

What a beautiful feeling that was to know that I wasn't right-handed. I was too sore to continue playing but I was forced to. "Walk it out man, stop being a little girl," the guys said. So, peer pressure led me to play two more games and then we went home. I put my hand in a cup of ice and went to bed.

That next morning I woke up and I could not raise my hand for the pain. I went to the hospital with my best friend Everette only to hear the following words from the doctor:

"You may have to wear this cast indefinitely or for at least two years. These brakes are normally the kind of brakes that end the careers of baseball players."

As I sat with the news from the doctor, I thought, Graduation is two months away and I am going to have to get a job right after I graduate –with my dream company Northern Telecom. They won't hire me with a broken arm. I couldn't even tie my shoelaces with out assistance. Who knows, maybe I want to get married. (*I thought I was ready*). I can't take notes or anything, what am I going to do?

Time was against me; I needed a mighty, powerful act from my Father and Creator.

Graduation was on the 24th of October. I went to my regular appointment on the eight of October, to get my stink cast changed. My Doctor felt the need to give me an x-ray and much to his surprise, my hand was in excellent condition.

The devil meant it for evil, but God meant it for my good. What a mighty God we serve?

Chapter Three: Graduation

On the 24th of October, I was about to take strides across the stage to receive my hard-earned diploma. I was the last name on the list to be called. My family had it planned. There would be a loud processional that included the whistles, the cowbells, the junkanoo drums, the roars, etc.
As I approached the Dean I kneeled down as they put the yellow and blue citation rope. Yes, I was the last name on the list to be called, but I graduated with the second highest honors (magna cum laude), within the top 600 black engineers in the U.S.A. and third in the class.

Finally, I achieved something that would pay my parents back for the heartache I might have caused them earlier. I saw it, I hugged my dad as we marched out, and he had to leave the room because he was crying. I couldn't believe I could have that effect on him, I never saw daddy cry. I felt extra special now.

The life that conquers is the life that moves
with a steady resolution and persistence

toward a predetermined goal. Those who
succeed are those who have thoroughly
learned the immense importance of plan in
life, and the tragic brevity of time.

—

That night I went home and had to get straight into
bed, my mouth and throat had developed some
kind of infection of blisters. I could not eat or
talk. Someone gave me orange juice to drink; I
took a chug and hollered because of the blistering
pain in my throat.

I returned home in Freeport, Grand Bahamas on
the 4th of November 1997 with my parents,
Chanika and LeBronze. During my time at home, I
could not get along with my parents at all. I
thought that being absent from home for such a
long time was the problem. Maybe mummy was
going through menopause. I didn't know the
reason at the time, but it was something. Perhaps
the real reason could be described through the
words of this poem.

Laughing gaily, yet hurting inside
I pushed back my tears & push forth my pride
"Are you okay" has been asked many times before
My only quick response was "Why do you ask" &
"Sure!"
I've often laid awake in the stillness of the night
Marveled by God's beauty and wonderful sight
Yet behind my mask of loneliness I hide
Whipping in the pain, hurt and anger I've cried
Many times I've been looked upon as a strong
spiritual saint
Who refuses to gloom or who has no complaints
Yet deep within lays my mask of broken pieces
That is in dyer need of a spiritual healing
Many times I'm called upon for servitude or
advice
Because I proudly present Christ as my life
Yet in my still-quiet corner I shun
All the many unanswered & rejected questions
Often throughout the day, I would sit still
To interact with God's sweet & calm-sense chill
The chill of His presence that surrounds me
Presenting the mask hidden is what I reveal

I've asked God for health & also strength
I've even asked Him to provide me with sufficient
wealth
I've asked for peace & joy that none can provide
But somehow my mask still lingers with stride
My hurt, my pain, my acquaint suffering
I've kept to myself time & time again
I've presented "a person" to one, few, & to many
But that person I've presented is not really me
-- Lynnette N. Gilbert, 6/14/99

In January, I got a call from Northern Telecom.
They wanted me - my dream company! This has
to be God. I prayed to work with this company
and I claimed it throughout my life at college. I
believed with my whole heart that I was going to
end up with this job. **When you want something
from God you must know how to ask for it and
see and speak those things as if they are. For He
said in His word, "Ask and it shall be given unto
you . . ."**

Chapter Four: The Real World

On the 16th of February 1998, I began working with Northern Telecom (NORTEL Fla.) as broadband marketing and sales engineer. I was real happy with my dream job. I was the first Bahamian with NORTEL. I called my father constantly and said, "Daddy you need to quit BaTelCo and get a real job."

During my third week there, I stayed at work late and on my way home, I began having a severe headache and seeing double. Every thing on the highway came and went in two's. I was scared as anything. I went home, jumped in the bed and slept praying that in the morning things would be better. But thing did not get better. Instead, I drove to work, which was a half-hour away, in the same condition. I immediately called my mother and told her what was happening.

She told me to go to an eye doctor. I told her I would go but I knew that I had to wait until payday, which was two weeks later. At this time the headaches were so bad that I was taking like ten to twelve headache pills a day, but nothing happened.

My dad had to come up from the Bahamas to attend a telecommunications seminar in Canada. Since he was going to change planes in Florida, I made plans to pick him up at the Miami International Airport. He had another flight to catch but I wanted him to see my apartment in Ft. Lauderdale. I was speeding heading north on the highway at speeds between 85 and 91 miles per hour. By the time we went to the apartment and looked around it was time for him to get back to the airport. I went into traffic again and came upon this string of cars. While in the car, we had the following dialogue:

Rondre: Maybe I could get around this traffic if I go off on the side of the road.

Daddy: Look out Ronni!!!!!

Rondre: What daddy, I am taking a shortcut.

Boom!!! I drove right over an underground manhole. I busted my tire but I kept on going.

Daddy: Pull over Ronni. You have a flat

Rondre: I don't feel it daddy

Eventually, we pulled into a gas station and called my cousin to pick us up. Although my dad was late, we made it right in time for the boarding call. I still loved my job. However, within one month my managers did an evaluation on my work status and I had scored poorly. They said that I was falling asleep on the job, coming to work with wrinkled clothing, speaking in an unmannerly fashion, chewing up my words (speaking with a slur). They called my parents about the matter and my father called me later that night and said that my managers thought that I might have been doing drugs. My dad said, "My son doesn't do drugs." I was in the kitchen cooking when I heard the phone ring. It was my dad calling to check on me.

Daddy: Hey Ronny, what you doing?"

Rondre: Cooking

Daddy: Huh?

Rondre: Cooking

Daddy: What?

Rondre: I am cooking daddy

Daddy: Oh, what you cooking

Rondre: Corn beef and rice

Daddy: What's that?

Rondre: Corn beef and rice daddy

Daddy: Ah let me call you back

It was a minutes after 8:00 p.m. on the 16th of March when I received the phone call. After eating I went to sleep. At 2:45 a.m. I heard banging at my door. It was my mother. I opened the door and started laughing.

Mommy: Why you laughing?

Rondre: Because you come knocking at my door so late.

She looked at me and said that I was leaning to the right and talking with a heavy slur. "You ain't going to work tomorrow, we are going to see a doctor." She had to call daddy to let him know she was in, but she couldn't dial direct from my phone so I told her to call 1-800-CALL-ATT.

Mommy: What?
Rondre: 1-800-CALL-ATT
Rondre: Mummy . . . 1-800-225-5288
Mommy: Dial it for me please

Now my mother has not had any known hearing problems. We were in the same room and I was in very close proximity to here when I repeated the phone number. Apparently, my slur was so bad that my mother could not pick out the words I said.

The next morning she phoned my managers at work for them to recommend a good family doctor. They recommended Dr. Maxine Hamilton and Dr. Solomon. Mommy called and set an appointment for 1:00 that afternoon, March 17th, 2000.

Chapter Five: At The Clinic

While waiting for Dr. Solomon, a nurse came to take my weight and pressure. Our conversation went a little like this.

Nurse: How much do you weigh sir?

Rondre: 170 lbs.

Nurse: Let's see!

Nurse: 141 lbs.

Rondre: Wow, I thought I was putting on weight

She put me in a room on a table to wait for Dr. Solomon. As the nurse left the room, I had a brief conversation with my mother.

Rondre: Mummy that woman retarded you know

Mommy: Why you say that?

Rondre: Cause she walks funny?

Mommy: Well what you think dey sayin' bout you?

Rondre: *Chuckle, Chuckle (I laughed but I really didn't find that funny though)*

Soon Dr. Solomon entered the room we were in and began the examination.

Dr. Solomon: Hi, how are you?

Mom & Dre: Fine thank you

Dr.: So how are you?

Rondre: Fine and you

Dr.: Have you been in here before, you look very familiar?

Rondre: No ma'am.

Dr.: Are you sure?

Rondre: Yes ma'am

Dr. O.K. I've seen you here before . . . Your mom tells me that you had vision problems

Rondre: Yes ma'am

Dr. How is your eyesight now?

Rondre: O.K.

Dr.: Let me see you walk, toe & heel (*I proceeded to walk on what I thought was my toes and heels.*)

Rondre: Chuckle! Chuckle! I can't do it

Dr.: O.K. let's see you walk on your tiptoes (*I tried again, this time walking on what I thought was my tiptoes.*)

Rondre: Wow, I can't do that either, I haven't exercised in a while

Dr.: O.K. let me see your reflexes

Rondre: Loud chuckle (my reflexes were really over active)

Dr.: What's the matter?

Rondre: That feels funny

Dr.: Do you always laugh like this?

Dre & Mom: Yes!! NO!!!!!!!

Rondre: Mummy, yes I always laugh like this

Dr.: Well there is definitely something wrong. I need you to go around the block to Broward General for further tests.

Mom: O.K. thank you Doc.

We left the clinic and went immediately to Broward General Hospital.

Chapter Six: Broward General Hospital

I sat in the waiting room with my mother for about two hours filling out insurance information and general information before they took me to the Emergency room (E.R). While in the ER the doctors performed a CT Scan. The results of the examination showed that I had a tumor in my brain. They stated that an M.R.I. needed to be done in order to get extensive details of the problem.

An M.R.I. was performed on the 19th of March and the results read as thus:

MRI REPORT

ADMITTING DIAGNOSIS: R/O BRAIN TUMOR

EXAM: MRI BRAIN W W/O CONTRAST

REASON FOR EXAM: AMS

EXAM DATE: MARCH 19, 1998

The mastoid air cells are clear. Inflammatory polyp is seen in the right maxillary sinus.

IMPRESSION:

DIFFUSE INFILTRATIVE TYPE MASS SEEN INVOLVING THE BRAIN STEM WITH

ENHANCEMENT. THE MASS IS LOCATED
IN THE BELLY OF THE PONS AND
EXTENDING INTO THE MID BRAIN AND
INTO THE LEFT CORTICAL SPINAL
TRACK AND POSTERIOR LIMB OF THE
INTERNAL CAPSULE.
FINDINGS ARE FELT TO REPRESENT
BRAIN STEM GLIOMA.

Based on the report, the doctors gave me a sentence of three to six months to live *with* treatment. Because the tumor was located on the brain and spinal cord, any manual operating would be a matter of life or death. Thus the stigma, the doctor's could not operate. The doctors recommended that I take thirty-five treatments of radiation (7 standard weeks) at 10:45 every morning and some chemo-therapy.

Transition One – Radiation
On the day of my first radiation treatment, the nurse came to prepare me and wheel me

downstairs. She started rejoicing and shouting. "I can feel the Holy Ghost all over you. You come from a praying Holy Ghost filled family. You tell that devil to go away because you are healed. In the state of mind I was in, I thought that maybe the lady was trippin'.

We got downstairs and she pointed, "That's your family there, I can see the Holy Ghost all over them. She had never met them before. **When God has His hand in business, don't bother to ask questions, just step aside and let Him work.**

I went into the radiation room and I was laid out on a table and my face was covered with a mask, which was screwed to the table in order to avoid movement. About halfway through the treatment I started to unscrew the mask because I felt as if I was suffocating. The radiologist dashed in to see that everything was ok.

Transition Two – Visitation
I remember my managers from Nortel –Tony

Huggins, and Stan Philips with Paul Ferguson came to visit me. I was working on a project before I left work. "Oh I have some details about the projects that I'm working on in my briefcase at work, I'll bring it to you tomorrow at the office," I said. "Don't worry about it Leon Jr.," Tony replied. I couldn't figure it out. These were the people who just had me in a meeting earlier this week. Apparently, I did not believe my condition was severe enough to keep me from doing my work.

The next day Dr. Solomon came to the hospital to check on me and she met my grandfather in my room.

Dr.: How are you Mr. Williams?

Grampy: I am fine and you

Dr.: Do you mind me asking, what is the relation?

Grampy: He is my grandson

Dr.: Now I see why I thought I knew him, wow

Apparently, my grandfather has been treated at this hospital some time ago, thus the relation question.

NOW IF ANYONE SEES THE RESEMBLANCE PLEASE LET ME KNOW, NOW!!!

I remember being visited by a nurse. We had a nice conversation and she told me not to worry about a thing. She also said that I would be out on the **thirtieth** of **March**. I kept telling my mom that I was going to come out on the thirtieth, but I couldn't come up with the name of the nurse. She had placed the discharge card on the wall and I showed it to my mother but she didn't see it. I thought, "Maybe my mom should be in here instead of me."

One evening one of my nurses, Elder Philmore Hughes, came in and told my parents, "Now its against work policy for me to be doing this but I informed my church staff about your son and I gave them the details and we put him forth in prayer. My parents were content.

One day while my grandparents visited I said "Grampy, all those people you prayed for and they were healed, why am I still here? Now what you gone do?" When I think back on that day, my mind reflects on a reading called "Breaking the Chains that Bind", by Lynnette Gilbert.

Looking up into the sky
the tears I rendered began to cry.
Crying out to my source of HELP
I fell to my knees, bowed my head & wept.
Crying, Lord how can I be free
from these chains of bondage that has captured
me!
Crying, "Lord, am I in this alone
fighting a war that is so harsh & cold?"
Then to my mind He placed in review
all those chains (of suffering) that were in
constitute.
He brought to my memory His beautiful promise
"Child I am with you always" - for I am not mine,
but I am His.
Whew!! A peaceful tear of smile began seeping

out

as my God removed my chain of doubt.

One by One I heard them fell

right back into the belly of hell.

The chains that held me emotionally stressed

fell to the ground as I rejoiced in God's strength.

The chains that held me physically strained

released its pressure so that I might breathe

again.

The chains that held me spiritually weak

disappeared and left me feeling humble & meek.

All those chains that had once imprisoned me

Are all gone; Now I am FREE!!

But WAIT!! This story has not come to an end

for there's more, much more to tell you, my dear

friends.

In order to keep these chains off hand

you must first come to understand.

With every problem that may arise

don't take it upon yourself, instead be wise.

Whenever distress may come your way

don't linger upon it for it may cause you to stray.

Whenever seeps of anger comes creeping in

don't act upon it & then sin.

Whenever temptation boldly walks into your life

alone you can't conquer its grief & strife.

Whenever upon you ailment begins to consume

prepare not the construction of your earthly tomb.

Instead, BREAK FREE your troubled mind a loose

and Jesus Christ will give you that extra spiritual

boost!

Place these chains in the hand of the one who

cares

who've witness every struggle & seen all tears.

Feed on the strength God offers you.

Embrace in His everlasting LOVE that is

righteous & true.

Praise Him now and forever more

and like the Tribe of Judah, ye shall conquer &

soar!!

Bonded chains which had hindered thee

shall be no more ~ for in Christ YOU ARE

FREE!!

by Lynnette Naomi Gilbert (5/14)

Later that week my grandfather sent my parents out the room and he and my grandmother prayed. He went out and told my parents that I was healed. On the 29th of March Dr. Solomon and Dr. Maxine Hamilton came to visit me and they said that by the looks of everything, I might be able to go home the following day.

Rondre: See mummy, I tell you the nurse said I could go on the thirtieth.

We have yet to find that nurse or any information on her . . .God works in mysterious ways, His wonders to perform. I spoke with a real life angel. Thank You God!!!

> *So shall they fear the name of the LORD*
> *from the west, and his glory from the rising*
> *of the sun. When the enemy shall come in*
> *like a flood, the Spirit of the LORD shall*
> *lift up a standard against him*
> *-Isaiah 59:19*

Transition Three – Home

I went home from the hospital and it was amazing.

The more medication and treatment I took, the younger I got. My mom watched me go through each of my childhood stages. All in all, I was happy to be out of the hospital. However, I still had a few weeks of chemotherapy to complete. One day my father and I went to the drive-thru of a famous fast food place after my treatment. "Daddy, I have to use the bathroom," I said.

"There's a bathroom on the inside," he answered. "I'll wait," I replied. When I couldn't wait any longer, I hurried on the inside. Just as I got in the front of a urinal, you guessed right. I leaked all over myself.

My mom, Chante, and LeBronze took turns bathing me, putting on my shoes and clothes, not necessarily in that order either. One day I was in the bathroom getting my balding hair (due to the radiation) cut by my mother. She said don't worry baby God is going to restore everything twofold. I said, "One hundred, two hundred, three hundred, four hundred, five hundred, six hundred, seven hundred, eight hundred, nine hundred, ten thousand. LeBronze laughed at me. **I didn't know at the time, but I was claiming my Victory, when you want a special work from God, you must claim it.**

I remember my Aunt Mickey calling me from California and she told me a story about a boy who drew a picture of his head and his tumor, and she wanted me to do that. I thought wow, "I can't write, much the less draw something and I am not artistic anyway." I have yet to do that drawing auntie but someday I'll get to it.

Chapter Seven: Easter Sunday

On Easter Sunday, Everett, Robert and his wife Tameisha, La-Tique, and my family went to Benny Hinn's healing service in Miami. At the end of the service my dad took me in line to wait to go on stage for prayers. We had to come back and sit down because my vision was shut-off and I was seeing black only.

My mom said that as she was praying for me, she felt a rush of fire from her legs up through her body. At the end of the service we were down on the floor giving time for traffic to clear up. We have a habit of being the last to leave any function, traffic or none. A woman came up to us from the stands. She said, **"I'm sorry but the Lord gave me a message to give to you, but I was hesitant. I was outside leaving and I had to come back inside because I had forgotten my keys. I noticed the love in this family and the Lord said to tell him that he is healed."** And my parents spoke with her for a while. *God wanted to get full glory for this manifestation.*

I went to my regular morning radiation treatment and the doctors felt the urge to perform another

M.R.I. on my brain. And much to their surprise, the tumor was gone. ***Praise the Lord, Praise the Lord, great things He has done.***

Chapter Eight: The Voyage Home

May 14, 1998- Wow I could not believe it. Fish, conch, tropical forests, THE BEACH, "boy this cruise ship needs to hurry," I said to myself. On the ship I made my sister, Chante, get up each time the buffet was open. As we were leaving one buffet, I stood up at the buffet stand picking cheese with my hands, one by one, and just stuffing my face. Boy, I was rude but I didn't realize it at the time.

When the ship docked we went to baggage claim and there was a banner on the wall that read **"WELCOME HOME RONDRE."** While walking past the sign I wondered to myself, "How do these people know me?" As soon as I stepped outside, members of the Bahama Brass Band and Youth band started up with a number. I couldn't figure out why the band would be playing at the harbor, so I just continued walking. My Aunt Connie had to stop me and take me back to the band. They played, but I wasn't feeling anything. Then my cousin Ikie told them, "Play satisfied, that's his song." They struck up with that song, I just smiled. I really couldn't figure out what all the excitement was all about. All that mattered to me is that I was home.

Our church was in the midst of having their youth convention. I was scheduled to speak sometime during the weekend. When the night came for me to speak, I walked into the church. I had never seen our church that full, with the exception of convention. I got scared. Later that night, I stood at the podium, for one minute without saying anything. Then I finally opened my mouth and said,

"It is good for a man that he bear the yoke in his youth.

My dad was just about to pull me off the stage. But I continued.

A yoke in the literal sense is a bar of wood so constructed as to unite two animals in, usually oxen, enabling them to work in the fields. Drawing loads and pulling instruments used in farming, such as the

plow, were the two chief works the yoke made possible. Also, used figuratively, the word yoke denotes a sense of servitude to the "law of God."

So, restated, the words of the prophet Jeremiah can be read, it is good for a man that he does the work of the Lord while in his youth. The Christian journey is not an easy one, especially for young people. But rather, it is one that is full of storms, trials, persecutions, and great tribulations. Sometimes things happen and you find yourself struggling wondering whether or not you can make it through. And you find yourself becoming fearful.

*But Jesus said in Matthew 11:29, "**Take my yoke upon you and learn of me; for I am meek and low in heart: and ye shall find rest unto your souls. For my yoke is easy and my burden is light.**" Why worry? Jesus promised that He would not put more on us than we can bear.*

What better example do we have than that

of Jesus Christ —who at the age of 12 was found in the temple amongst the doctors doing the work of His father. "It is good for a man that he bear the yoke in his youth."

God has a ministry for each one of us. And it is important for us as young people that we be attentive to the Spirit's direction. Although we may not all have the same calling, we all have one common goal, and that is to do the will of Him. The service of the Lord is one that we should do with utmost willingness; for it is only then that we will find rest. The yoke will be easy and the burden will be light. However, when we do God's work hesitantly, we find that the yoke tightens and the burdens become heavy.

Bearing the Yoke in your Youth

Why has God chosen you and I? Why does God want to use young people to do His work? Why should we have to bear the yoke? The apostle John writes in 1 John 2:14, **I have written unto you, young men, because ye are strong, and the word of God abideth in you, and ye have overcome the wicked one**.

And Saul said to David, Thou art not able to go against the Philistine to fight with Him: For thou art but a youth, and he a man of war from his youth. David said moreover, The Lord that delivered me out of the paw of the lion, and out of the paw of the bear, He will deliver me out of the hand of the Philistine. And Saul said unto David, Go and the Lord be with thee. David was bearing the yoke in his youth. Throughout history, people have been fighting battles. The teenager is no exception. Much of the teens life is lived in the place we call the battle zone. For the

teenager, these battles are peer pressure,
identity crisis, family problems, friendship,
school and even church. The devil comes
with one thing in mind and that is to
devour whomever he can –especially our
young people. He uses such things as
drugs, alcohol, sex, the love of money and
many other things that may seem
appealing to young persons –things that
we feel may bring us joy and happiness.
But I want you to know that these things
only bring destruction. We can't yield to
the things of this world. I have written
unto you, young men because ye are
strong, and the word of God abideth in
you, and ye have overcome the wicked one.
So when the storms rise and Satan begins
to throw his fiery darts at you, shout out,
In the name of Jesus, I have the victory.
Tell me who can stand before me when I
call on that great name. Jesus, Jesus,
precious Jesus, I have the victory. It is
good for a man that he bear the yoke in his

youth.

*Youth can and must make a difference.
God has chosen us and is depending on us
to impact this decadent society. Most
people who accept Christ's redemption are
going to do so while they are young. The
influence of young Christian people is
more likely to have an effect upon them
than will that of those whom they feel
cannot identify with their generation.
People need the Lord! Love for these
people is the only compelling force that
assures consistency in a young persons
outreach ministry. Christ is our perfect
example. While feeling responsible to keep
those who had been given Him, He kept
them by keeping them involved with him as
He researched out compassionately to
hurting people. Reach out to people is our
business.*

*God loves persons – Individuals. They
come into this world one at a time. And
they are born again one at the time as the*

Spirit deals with them individually.
Spiritual growth occurs according to an
individual's personal response to the
Spirit's prompting. As young people, we
must be attentive to the Spirit's direction
and the only way we can do this is by
becoming a praying, listening people who
will hear what God is saying to us now.
We Must Bear the Yoke in your Youth.
Christ had a great mandate. In Luke 4:18
*he says, "**The Spirit of the Lord is upon***
me, for He hath anointed me to preach
the gospel to the poor. He hath sent me to
heal the brokenhearted, to preach
deliverance to the captives, and the
recovering of sight to the blind, to set at
liberty them that are bruised. To preach
the acceptable year of the Lord. *"*
When it comes to presenting the gospel,
communication is what counts. Methods of
communication vary. While one method
may be highly effective in one situation,
some other method may be more effective

in another.

Sad to say, but we are loosing a lot of our young people because of miscommunication. We don't know how to speak from one youth to another. As young people, we need to present the message at any method and we must come by all means that we may win some. It is good for a man that he bear the yoke in his youth.

The harvest is full of young, ripe souls. If we fail to reap them while they are young, the chances of them knowing the Lord diminishes greatly in succeeding years. Virtually all children have a period of vulnerability when they will believe anything they have been taught. For example, children who are between two and five years old will readily accept the notion that Santa Claus can fly over all the world on a single night, and deliver gifts to chimneys to every good person.

Our or your offspring will unquestionable

adopt the spiritual values we impart to
them during these important years. That
they respond more readily to the gospel while they
are young is of divine design.
As we recognize that God has so ordered
it, wisdom teaches us the importance of
working with God in this great end time
harvest.
That's why the bible says, "Train up a
child in the way he should go and when he
is old he will not depart from it." We will
train them or we will loose them!
These are crucial years, years when
decisions are made which will determine
the course they will follow for a lifetime.
Train them and you we have laborers for
the harvest. Fail to train them and we will
loose a generation.
It is a generation upon whom the end of
the world will come. God is touching the
hearts of this generation. He is also rising
up laborers who will engage themselves
with Jesus in that which is dearest to His

heart. God is depending on us to impact
this decadent society.
It's a different generation. Our world is
changing. The pressures we feel are real
and we need special guidance. This
cannot come from just anyone, but from
someone whom we trust and respect.
Young people are facing troubled times.
Many kids today, some of you know
personally, are in crisis. As their friends,
brothers and sisters, parents and youth
ministers: What can we say to them? Will
they listen to us? Can we reach through to
them? Is there a way to reach through to
them? Is there a way to help them through
their problems? Or better yet, can we
reach them before a crisis takes place?
We can't remove all the problems in their
lives, but we can learn how to help them
through troubled times with strong
spiritual guidance. What's more, we can
introduce to them a friend that sticks
closer than a brother and lead them into a

relationship with Jesus Christ.
I spoke mainly to the parents this morning,
but tonight I am speaking to our leaders.
We need to reposition ourselves. We are
living in a day and age where it seems as if
anything goes. Leaders, we need to be
able to lead our young people to that
comfort zone in Christ and the only way we
can do this is by constantly consulting with
God for His direction, His guidance and
strength.

Young people the word of God says, "In
the last days..." and in another portion it
says, "Where there is no vision..." Without
us, all of this can easily diminish.
In closing, I want to say to the leaders that
we are responsible for teaching the way. If
we are going to lead, we are going to have
to walk circumspectly and let God order
our steps. If we live in the spirit let us also
walk in the spirit.
I don't know how many people understood me

with my speech slur, but if one soul was saved, that is all that counts. There were people who looked at me, heard me speak and said, "he is still sick, God ain't do nuttin' for him." I weighed about 210 lbs and looked like a monster, and how I spoke was incomprehensible to many.

But if God had allowed me to return in a normal fashion, the people would have doubted that I was sick in the first place. *I THOUGHT THAT IT WAS THE PHARISEES ONLY, WHO LOOKED FOR SIGNS.*

Chapter Nine: The Rand Memorial Hospital

My mom weaned me off of the medication and I started to see how I really looked. I was a slob. I just stopped eating; everything that I ate would just come back up. And I ended up in the rand for 4 days being examined for gastritis.

I had lost over 40 lbs in one month. I was suffering from nasty stomach pains and my mom said that I was pregnant. **I was smart enough to know that if you get pregnant your stomach gets bigger not smaller. Wow and I didn't even take a course of pregnancy 101, Mummy.**

Well, the Lord healed me from that and I went home. A month or two later, my friend in Atlanta flew me up to play drums on her album God's Offer. In previous years I thought she was crazy but after this stunt, I knew she was crazy. I hadn't played drums in over a year. Prior to taking the trip, she always called me saying, "You'd better practice because you're playing on my album." One day I got enough courage and asked my father to take me down to the church so I could play the drums. After playing a beat or two, I fell off the drum set with a big **BOOM!!!** I had no timing. I could not keep myself balanced enough to play for an entire recording session. I also knew that she would not take "no" for an answer, so into the plane I went.

My best friend Everette accompanied me at the studio. With lots of prayers and support, I got through the recording session with a few errors. I give God all the praise and glory for his miraculous works.

Soon after, I flew back home to Freeport reinspired to continue my job search. I was persistent for several weeks. Then weeks turned into months.

Applying for job after job, interview after interview, and I got no job. I started to feel as if I was a let down, all that money my parents spent on me for high school and college, and I can't get a simple job.

Furthermore, I have a lot of friends who weren't afforded the opportunity to go to

college but they are making all the money. I said to God, "Lord, I had a job why did you let me get sick and heal me, only to return home for two years and not be able to get a job. Lord, you are a waste of time."

God answered me, in the psychiatric ward I went.

"...For most of life, nothing wonderful happens. If you don't enjoy getting up and working and finishing your work and sitting down to a meal with family or friends, then the chances are that you're not going to be very happy. If someone bases his happiness or unhappiness on major events like a great new job, huge amounts of money, a flawlessly happy marriage or a trip to Paris, that person isn't going to be happy much of the time. If, on the other hand, happiness depends on a good breakfast,

flowers in the yard, a drink or a
nap, then we are more likely to live
with quite a bit of happiness."
- Andy Rooney

I spent my birthday, December 30, 1999, in the DI ward. It was the absolutely scariest time of my life. I was hallucinating and seeing things that I wish not to discuss at the time. **With all that God had brought me out of, I had thrown all back in His face. I had forgotten that without God I am nothing.**

Botanists say that trees need the
powerful March winds to flex their
trunks and main branches, so that
the sap is drawn up to nourish the
budding leaves. Perhaps we need
the gales of life in the same way,
though we dislike enduring them. A
blustery period in our fortunes
is often the prelude to a new spring
of life and health, success and
happiness, when we keep steadfast
in faith and look to the good in

-73-

spite of appearances.

- Jane Truax

While at the DI Ward, one doctor looked at the scans that I had done in Florida and he could not believe it. "This is amazing," he said. I am writing a book and I am going to put him in it. God brought me out of a situation once more, regardless of the way I acted or the things I said. **God is not a God of spite and he puts everything into the sea of forgetfulness when you find your way back to Him.**

Chapter Ten: The Present

A few months later, March 2000 I attended our National Convention (Church of God of Prophecy) in Nassau, and my Godfather Clarence N. Williams offered me a job as an accountant apprentice. A few weeks later my father and I were speaking with Dr. Kevin Alcino and I was sharing with him my experience. He told me to give him my resume and that he would see whether or not there is anything available.

I attended the Ernest St. Church of God of Prophecy under the patronage of Bishop Samuel Alleyne where I now serve as Assistant Youth Minister.

Later I got a call from Winston Rolle of Bahamas Copier saying that he wanted me to come in for an interview. I went and a few weeks later, I received a letter offering me the position of **Project Manager** with the addition of **Software Support.**

I GIVE GOD ALL THE PRAISE, THANKS, AND GLORY. FOR WHEN HE DOES SOMETHING IT IS WELL DONE.

I want to do my best in service for Him because when it is all said and done, I want to hear him say, **"Well done thou good and faithful servant, thou has been faithful over few things, I will make thee ruler over many things."**

Yes I am only twenty-four but I have experienced enough to know GOD is real. I have felt Him time and time again. And if you want to experience the same thing I have experienced, you need to open up your heart, your mind your spirit to Him.
I am young, but David was young when he slew Goliath, Joseph was young when his dreams came true, Daniel was young when he stood in the lion's den, the three Hebrew boys were young when they stood in the fiery furnace.

I call upon you young men because ye are strong, and the word of God abideth in you, and ye have overcome the wicked one.

Young people we are living in troubled times. We are facing crucial years. Years when we will make decisions that will determine our course of action for a lifetime. Get involved in church and Godly activities for it is one of the only things that will assure consistency in our outreach ministry as young Christians.

I pray that at least one person that reads the words on these pages will be enlightened, enriched, encouraged continuing in his or her Christian service. I also pray that person will never wavering or feeling weary. But instead, that they will press toward the mark for the prize of the high calling, which is in *Jesus* our Lord.

Now unto Him who is able to keep you from falling and to present you faultless before the presence of His glory with exceeding joy. To the only wise God our Savior, be glory and majesty, dominion and power, both now and ever. Amen.
Jude 1:24,25

www.ingramcontent.com/pod-product-compliance
Lightning Source LLC
Chambersburg PA
CBHW021910040426
42447CB00007B/790